Social Security

Made Simple And Easy To Understand 2024

Property of

Elysian Sage

Dedication

This guide is dedicated to all those who strive for a secure and dignified future.

To the hardworking individuals who have contributed to the Social Security system, both through their labor and their advocacy, this guide is for you. Your dedication and commitment to building a better future for all Americans inspire us every day.

To the retirees who have paved the way for future generations, this guide honors your contributions and sacrifices. Your resilience and wisdom serve as a beacon of hope for those navigating their own retirement journey.

To the individuals with disabilities who face unique challenges yet continue to persevere with grace and determination, this guide stands as a testament to your strength and resilience. Your courage and perseverance inspire us to strive for a more inclusive and compassionate society.

To the survivors who have endured loss and grief, yet continue to find strength and hope in the face of adversity, this guide acknowledges your resilience and offers support and solidarity. Your resilience and determination are a source of inspiration to us all.

To the advocates and champions of Social Security who tirelessly work to protect and expand this vital program, this guide recognizes your tireless efforts and unwavering commitment to social justice. Your advocacy and dedication are essential to ensuring that all Americans have access to the resources they need for a secure and dignified future.

This guide is dedicated to each and every individual who believes in the power of Social Security to uplift and empower individuals, families, and communities. May we continue to work together to build a future where everyone can thrive with dignity and security.

With deepest gratitude and appreciation,

Elysian Sage .

TABLE OF CONTENTS

A PERSONAL JOURNEY

Before we take off, allow me to share with you a story that illustrates the profound impact of Social Security on individuals and families.

As a Social Security advisor, I've had the privilege of witnessing firsthand the transformative power of this vital program in the lives of countless individuals. But there's one story that stands out among the rest – a story that encapsulates the essence of Social Security and its profound impact on those it serves.

Meet Sarah. A vibrant woman in her early sixties, Sarah had spent the better part of her life dedicated to her career as a teacher. From shaping young minds in the classroom to fostering a sense of community within her school, Sarah's passion for education knew no bounds. But as retirement loomed on the horizon, Sarah found herself grappling with a mix of excitement and apprehension. Would she have enough savings to live comfortably in her golden years? What would retirement look like without the familiar routine of lesson plans and school bells?

It was during this period of uncertainty that Sarah reached out to me for guidance on navigating the complexities of Social

Security. Sitting across from her, I could sense the weight of her worries as she poured out her concerns about the future. Would she be able to afford her medical expenses? What if she faced unexpected challenges in retirement?

Together, we delved into the intricacies of Social Security, exploring the various benefits available to Sarah as a retired educator. As we pored over her earnings record and calculated her potential benefits, a sense of relief washed over Sarah's face. It was as if a burden had been lifted from her shoulders, replaced by a newfound sense of security and reassurance.

But our journey didn't end there. With each passing day, Sarah's confidence in her financial future grew stronger. Armed with a deeper understanding of Social Security and its nuances, she embarked on her retirement with a sense of purpose and peace of mind.

Fast forward a few years, and I received a letter from Sar filled with gratitude for the guidance and support she had received. In her words, Social Security had been more than just a financial safety net – it had been a lifeline, providing her with the stability and security she needed to embrace this new chapter of her life with open arms.

Sarah's story serves as a poignant reminder of the profound impact of Social Security on individuals and families across the nation. From teachers to truck drivers, nurses to firefighters, Social Security touches the lives of millions, offering a beacon of hope in times of uncertainty and a foundation for a brighter future.

* * *

As a Social Security advisor, it's stories like Sarah's that fuel my passion for helping others navigate the complexities of this vital program. Because at the end of the day, Social Security isn't just about numbers on a page – it's about people, their hopes, their dreams, and their journey toward a more secure tomorrow.

1. Introduction to Social Security

Since the dawn of civilization, communities have grappled with the profound questions of care and security for their members. From ancient tribes to modern nations, the concept of looking after one another during times of need has remained a fundamental pillar of societal structure. Now, imagine a safety net that spans across an entire nation, offering support and stability to millions of individuals and families in their golden years, during periods of disability, or in the aftermath of a loved one's passing. This safety net is what we call Social Security.

Picture this: you've spent decades working hard, contributing your time, energy, and skills to your job, your community, and your country. As you approach the twilight of your career, thoughts of retirement begin to dance in your mind. But amidst the anticipation of newfound freedom and relaxation, there may also be a flicker of uncertainty. How will you support yourself financially once you stop working? Will you have enough savings to live comfortably? What if unforeseen circumstances, such as illness or injury, derail your plans?

This is where Social Security steps in, like a dependable friend offering a helping hand in times of need. At its core, Social

Security is a government program designed to provide financial assistance to individuals who are retired, disabled, or survivors of deceased workers. It's a safety net woven with the threads of compassion, solidarity, and foresight, ensuring that no one is left behind in their time of need.

But what exactly does Social Security entail? Let's break it down into bite-sized pieces, shall we?

First and foremost, Social Security encompasses a variety of benefits tailored to different life circumstances. There are retirement benefits, which serve as a financial cushion for individuals who have reached the end of their working years. Then there are disability benefits, offering support to those who find themselves unable to work due to a qualifying disability. And let's not forget about survivor benefits, providing assistance to the loved ones left behind in the wake of a worker's death.

But eligibility for these benefits isn't granted indiscriminately. Like any well-organized system, Social Security has its criteria and requirements. Age, work history, income level – these factors all come into play when determining who qualifies for which benefits. And while the process may seem daunting at first glance, fear not! Navigating the ins and outs of Social Security is a journey we'll embark on together, hand in hand.

Now, you might be wondering, how exactly does one go about enrolling in Social Security benefits? Is it a labyrinthine maze of paperwork and bureaucracy, or a straightforward path to financial security? Fear not, dear reader, for the answer lies somewhere in between. With the advent of modern technology, applying for Social Security benefits has become more accessible than ever. Whether you prefer the convenience of online applications or the personal touch of face-to-face interactions, there's a method that suits your needs.

But Social Security isn't just about receiving benefits – it's also about understanding them. From calculating your retirement income to maximizing your disability benefits, knowledge is power when it comes to navigating the intricacies of this vital program. And as your trusted advisor in all things Social Security, it's my mission to equip you with the tools and information you need to make informed decisions about your financial future.

So, whether you're just dipping your toes into the waters of Social Security or diving in headfirst, know that you're not alone on this journey. Together, we'll unravel the mysteries of retirement, disability, and survivor benefits, one step at a time. Welcome to the world of Social Security – where compassion meets financial security, and your peace of mind is our top priority.

Certainly! Let's delve into the world of Social Security.

1.1 What is Social Security?

Social Security. The term often conjures up images of retirement checks and government bureaucracy. But what lies beneath the surface of this seemingly mundane phrase? What exactly is Social Security, and why does it matter?

At its core, Social Security is a cornerstone of the American social safety net – a system of programs designed to provide financial assistance to individuals and families during times of need. Established in the depths of the Great Depression, Social Security emerged as a beacon of hope in an era marked by economic turmoil and uncertainty.

But Social Security is more than just a government program. It's a promise – a promise to uphold the dignity and well-being of every American, regardless of age, income, or circumstance. It's a testament to the idea that, in the wealthiest nation on earth, no one should be left to fend for themselves in times of hardship.

So, what does Social Security encompass, exactly? Well, it's a multifaceted system that offers a range of benefits to eligible individuals. From retirement checks for seniors to disability payments for those unable to work, Social Security serves as a lifeline for millions of Americans across the country. But perhaps most importantly, it provides a sense of security – a safety net that ensures no one falls through the cracks.

1.2 Purpose and Importance

But why is Social Security so important? What purpose does it serve in the grand scheme of things?

To understand the significance of Social Security, we must first recognize the harsh realities that many Americans face. For far too many, retirement is not a golden age of leisure and relaxation, but rather a period of financial uncertainty and anxiety. Without the security provided by Social Security, countless seniors would be left to fend for themselves, grappling with the harsh realities of poverty and deprivation.

But it's not just seniors who benefit from Social Security. The program also provides crucial support to individuals with disabilities and survivors of deceased workers. For those unable to work due to a qualifying disability, Social Security Disability Insurance offers a financial lifeline, ensuring that they can maintain their dignity and independence despite their limitations. And for the loved ones left behind in the wake of a worker's passing, survivor benefits offer a measure of financial security in the midst of grief and loss.

But perhaps the most profound impact of Social Security lies in its ability to foster a sense of solidarity and compassion among all Americans. In a society often characterized by division and discord, Social Security serves as a reminder that we are all in this together – that we have a collective responsibility to care for one another, especially in times of need.

So, why does Social Security matter? Because it embodies the values that define us as a nation – values of compassion, solidarity, and dignity for all. It's a testament to the idea that, by working together and supporting one another, we can create a brighter, more secure future for generations to come. And in a world fraught with uncertainty, that's a promise worth fighting for.

1.3 Historical Development

To truly understand the significance of Social Security, we must journey back in time to the tumultuous era of the Great Depression. In the 1930s, America was in the grip of an economic crisis unlike anything it had ever seen. Millions were out of work, families were struggling to make ends meet, and the specter of poverty loomed large over the nation.

It was against this backdrop of despair that the seeds of Social Security were planted. In 1935, President Franklin D. Roosevelt signed the Social Security Act into law, marking a watershed moment in American history. The Act aimed to provide economic security to the elderly, the disabled, and the unemployed through a system of social insurance.

At its inception, Social Security primarily focused on retirement benefits for seniors. Workers would contribute a portion of their earnings to the Social Security trust fund through payroll taxes, and in return, they would receive a monthly benefit upon reaching retirement age. This revolutionary concept represented a fundamental shift in how America approached the issue of poverty and old age.

Over the years, Social Security has evolved and expanded to meet the changing needs of society. In the 1950s and 1960s, disability benefits were added to provide support to individuals who were unable to work due to physical or mental impairments. Later, survivor benefits were introduced to assist the families of deceased workers, ensuring that they could maintain a basic standard of living after the loss of a loved one.

Today, Social Security stands as one of the most successful and enduring social programs in American history. It has lifted millions of seniors out of poverty, provided a lifeline to individuals with disabilities, and offered a measure of security to families in their darkest hours. But its journey is far from over – as we look to the future, Social Security continues to evolve, adapt, and innovate in order to meet the needs of a changing society.

1.4 Social Security Administration: Roles and Responsibilities

At the helm of the Social Security program stands the Social Security Administration (SSA) – a federal agency tasked with overseeing the administration of benefits and services to millions of Americans. Founded in 1935 alongside the Social Security Act, the SSA plays a pivotal role in ensuring that the promises of Social Security are upheld for generations to come.

But what exactly does the SSA do? At its core, the SSA is responsible for a wide range of duties related to the administration of Social Security benefits. This includes everything from processing benefit applications and determining eligibility to issuing payments and managing the Social Security trust fund.

In addition to its administrative functions, the SSA also plays a crucial role in educating the public about Social Security and its various programs. Through outreach initiatives, educational materials, and online resources, the SSA works tirelessly to ensure that Americans have the information they need to make informed decisions about their benefits.

But perhaps most importantly, the SSA serves as a beacon of hope and support for millions of Americans in their time of need. Whether it's helping a senior retire with dignity, providing financial assistance to a disabled individual, or offering solace to a grieving family, the SSA is there every step of the way, fulfilling its mission to serve the American people with compassion and integrity.

2. Understanding Social Security Benefits

Social Security benefits are the cornerstone of the program, providing financial support to millions of Americans in various stages of life. Understanding the different types of benefits available is crucial to maximizing the assistance provided by Social Security. Let's explore the various types of Social Security benefits in detail:

2.1 Types of Social Security Benefits

Retirement Benefits

Retirement benefits are perhaps the most well-known aspect of Social Security. These benefits are designed to provide a steady source of income to individuals who have reached retirement age and have paid into the Social Security system throughout their working years. The age at which you become eligible for full retirement benefits depends on your birth year, but it typically ranges from 65 to 67 years old.

To qualify for retirement benefits, you must have accumulated enough "credits" by working and paying Social Security taxes. These credits are based on your earnings, and most people need 40 credits (equivalent to about 10 years of work) to qualify for retirement benefits.

Retirement benefits are calculated based on your average lifetime earnings, with higher earners receiving higher benefits. You can choose to start receiving benefits as early as age 62, but doing so will result in a reduced monthly benefit. Conversely, delaying retirement can increase your benefit amount.

Disability Benefits

Social Security Disability Insurance (SSDI) provides crucial financial support to individuals who are unable to work due to a qualifying disability. To qualify for disability benefits, you must have a medical condition that prevents you from engaging in substantial gainful activity and is expected to last at least one year or result in death.

The process of applying for disability benefits can be complex, involving medical evaluations, documentation of your disability, and assessments of your ability to work. If approved, you will receive monthly disability payments to help cover living expenses and medical costs.

Survivor Benefits

Survivor benefits are available to the spouses, children, and other dependents of deceased workers who were covered by Social Security. These benefits provide financial support to help families cope with the loss of a loved one and maintain their standard of living.

Survivor benefits may include a one-time lump sum death payment, monthly survivor benefits for spouses and dependent children, and even benefits for divorced spouses in certain circumstances. Eligibility for survivor benefits depends on various factors, including the deceased worker's earnings history and the relationship between the survivor and the deceased.

Spousal Benefits

Spousal benefits are available to the spouses of retired or disabled workers who are eligible for Social Security benefits. These benefits allow spouses who have not worked or earned enough credits on their own to receive a portion of their spouse's Social Security benefits.

To qualify for spousal benefits, you must be at least 62 years old and have been married to your spouse for at least one year. The amount of spousal benefits you receive is typically based on your spouse's earnings history and the age at which you claim benefits.

Dependent Benefits

Dependent benefits are available to certain family members of retired, disabled, or deceased workers who are eligible for Social Security benefits. These benefits provide financial support to spouses, children, and other dependents who rely on the income of the Social Security beneficiary.

Dependent benefits may include monthly payments for spouses caring for children under the age of 16, benefits for disabled adult children, and even benefits for dependent parents in some cases. The eligibility criteria and amount of dependent benefits vary depending on the specific circumstances of the beneficiary and their family members.

Understanding the various types of Social Security benefits available is essential for maximizing the support provided by the program. Whether you're planning for retirement, coping with a disability, or navigating the loss of a loved one, Social Security benefits can offer a crucial source of financial stability and peace of mind.

2.2 Eligibility Criteria for Each Benefit Type

Understanding the eligibility criteria for each type of Social Security benefit is essential for individuals seeking assistance from the program. Here's a breakdown of the eligibility requirements for the different benefit types:

Retirement Benefits:

To be eligible for retirement benefits, you must:

- Have reached the minimum age for retirement (typically between 62 and 67, depending on your birth year).
- Have earned enough "credits" by working and paying Social Security taxes.
- Be fully retired or earning below the earnings limit set by Social Security if you choose to receive benefits before reaching full retirement age.
- Not be receiving certain other types of Social Security benefits, such as disability benefits.

Disability Benefits:

- To qualify for Social Security Disability Insurance (SSDI) benefits, you must:
- Have a medical condition that prevents you from engaging in substantial gainful activity (SGA) and is expected to last for at least one year or result in death.

- Have earned enough work credits based on your age at the time of disability onset.
- Meet the SSA's definition of disability, which includes being unable to perform work you did before and being unable to adjust to other work due to your medical condition.

Survivor Benefits:

To be eligible for survivor benefits, you must:

- Be the spouse, child, or dependent parent of a deceased worker who was covered by Social Security.
- Meet certain age and relationship requirements.
- Not be currently married (for spouses) or earning above the earnings limit set by Social Security (for surviving spouses who remarry before age 60).

Spousal Benefits:

To qualify for spousal benefits, you must:

- Be the spouse of a retired, disabled, or deceased worker who is eligible for Social Security benefits.
- Be at least 62 years old.
- Have been married to your spouse for at least one year prior to applying for benefits (with exceptions for certain divorced spouses).

Dependent Benefits:

Eligibility for dependent benefits varies depending on the relationship between the beneficiary and the worker who is eligible for Social Security benefits. Common eligibility criteria include:

- Being the child, stepchild, or adopted child of a retired, disabled, or deceased worker.
- Being unmarried and under a certain age limit (usually 18 or 19, or 22 if a full-time student).
- Being disabled before reaching age 22 and meeting the SSA's definition of disability.

2.3 Benefits for Non-Citizens and Expatriates

Social Security benefits are not limited to U.S. citizens. Non-citizens who meet the eligibility criteria outlined above may also qualify for benefits, provided they have worked in the United States and paid Social Security taxes.

Additionally, U.S. citizens who are living abroad, commonly referred to as expatriates, may still be eligible for Social Security benefits. However, eligibility requirements and benefit amounts may vary depending on factors such as the length of time spent working in the United States and the specific provisions of any bilateral Social Security agreements between the U.S. and the country of residence.

As a professional Social Security advisor, it's important to stay informed about the eligibility criteria and benefit options available to individuals from diverse backgrounds and circumstances. By understanding the nuances of Social Security eligibility, we can better assist clients in navigating the complexities of the program and accessing the benefits they deserve.

3. Enrollment and Application Process

The journey towards accessing Social Security benefits begins with understanding who exactly can apply for this invaluable support system. Let's embark on this enlightening expedition together, shall we?

3.1 Who Can Apply for Social Security Benefits?

Now, you might be wondering, "Who exactly is eligible to apply for Social Security benefits?" Well, dear reader, the answer may surprise you – because the truth is, Social Security benefits are not limited to a select few. In fact, a wide range of individuals may qualify for assistance through this vital program.

First and foremost, let's talk about retirement benefits. Retirement – the golden years, the twilight of one's career, the well-deserved reward for a lifetime of hard work. If you find yourself longing for the serene shores of retirement, then Social Security benefits may be just the ticket to help you embark on this new chapter of your life with confidence and peace of mind.

But retirement benefits are just the tip of the iceberg when it comes to Social Security eligibility. Individuals with disabilities – whether physical or mental – may also be eligible for assistance through Social Security Disability Insurance (SSDI). If you find yourself unable to work due to a qualifying disability, then SSDI benefits could provide you with the financial support you need to navigate life's challenges with dignity and independence.

And let's not forget about survivor benefits. The bittersweet embrace of love and loss. If you are the spouse, child, or dependent parent of a deceased worker who was covered by Social Security, then survivor benefits may offer you a lifeline in the midst of grief and uncertainty. Whether you're coping with the loss of a beloved partner or supporting a family member through their darkest hour, Social Security benefits can provide much-needed stability and support during trying times.

But wait, there's more! Social Security benefits aren't just for retirees, individuals with disabilities, and survivors – they're also available to certain family members of eligible workers. Spouses, children, and even dependent parents may be eligible for benefits based on the earnings record of a retired, disabled, or deceased worker. So, if you find yourself in need of financial assistance and have a qualifying relationship to a Social Security beneficiary, then don't hesitate to explore your options for benefits.

Intrigued? I certainly hope so! The world of Social Security benefits is vast and multifaceted, offering a lifeline to individuals and families in various stages of life. So, whether you're dreaming of retirement, grappling with a disability, or navigating the aftermath of loss, remember – you're not alone on this journey. Social Security benefits are here to offer you the support and security you deserve, every step of the way.

3.2 How to Apply for Benefits

A beacon of financial security and stability in an uncertain world. But how does one go about applying for these invaluable lifelines? Fear not, dear reader, for I am here to guide you through the process with grace and clarity.

Online Application Process

In this modern age of technology, applying for Social Security benefits has never been easier – thanks to the wonders of the internet! With just a few clicks of your mouse or taps of your finger, you can complete your application from the comfort of your own home, at a time that suits your schedule.

To begin the online application process, simply visit the official Social Security Administration (SSA) website. Once there, you'll find a wealth of resources and information to help you navigate the process with ease. From detailed guides and tutorials to helpful FAQs, the SSA website is your one-stop shop for all things Social Security.

Once you're ready to begin your application, you'll be prompted to create a personal my Social Security account. This account allows you to access your Social Security information online, track the status of your application, and receive important updates and notifications from the SSA.

Once your account is set up, you can begin the application process by providing the required information and documentation. This may include details about your work history, earnings, and personal information, as well as any supporting documentation related to your eligibility for benefits.

Once your application is submitted, you can track its progress and receive updates on its status through your my Social Security account. And before you know it, you'll be well on your way to accessing the benefits you need to support yourself and your loved ones.

In-Person Application

But what if you prefer the personal touch of face-to-face interaction when applying for Social Security benefits? Fear not, for the option of in-person application is still available to you.

To apply for benefits in person, simply visit your nearest Social Security office. There, you'll find a team of dedicated professionals ready to assist you every step of the way. From answering your questions and providing guidance on the application process to helping you gather the necessary documentation, the staff at your local Social Security office are here to ensure that your application experience is smooth and seamless.

When visiting the Social Security office, be sure to bring along any required documentation, such as proof of identity, citizenship, and work history. This will help expedite the application process and ensure that your application is processed accurately and efficiently.

Once your application is submitted, you can expect to receive updates on its status through mail or phone. And before you know it, you'll be on your way to receiving the benefits you need to support yourself and your loved ones – all thanks to the power of Social Security.

So whether you choose to apply online or in person, rest assured that the process is designed to be as accessible and user-friendly as possible. With a little guidance and support, you'll be well on your way to accessing the benefits you deserve in no time.

3.3 Required Documentation and Information

Behold, the final piece of the puzzle in our journey towards accessing Social Security benefits – the all-important documentation and information required to complete the application process. Let's delve into this crucial aspect with clarity and confidence.

Required Documentation and Information

When it comes to applying for Social Security benefits, having the right documentation and information at your fingertips is essential. After all, the Social Security Administration (SSA) needs to verify your identity, work history, and eligibility for benefits before they can begin processing your application.

So, what exactly do you need to gather before you embark on this important journey? Let's break it down, shall we?

Personal Identification

First and foremost, you'll need to provide proof of your identity. This typically includes documents such as:

- A valid government-issued photo ID (e.g., driver's license or passport).

- Your original birth certificate or a certified copy.

- Proof of U.S. citizenship or lawful immigration status (if applicable).

These documents serve as the foundation of your application, verifying who you are and ensuring that you are eligible to apply for Social Security benefits.

Work History

Next up, you'll need to provide information about your work history and earnings. This helps the SSA determine your eligibility for benefits and calculate the amount you're entitled to receive. Here's what you'll need to gather:

- Your Social Security number (SSN) or a copy of your Social Security card.

- W-2 forms or self-employment tax returns covering your earnings for each year you worked.

- Any other documentation of income, such as pay stubs or tax records, if W-2 forms are not available.

Be sure to gather documentation for all the years you worked, as this will ensure that your benefit amount is accurately calculated based on your lifetime earnings.

Medical Records (for Disability Benefits)

If you're applying for Social Security Disability Insurance (SSDI) benefits, you'll also need to provide documentation of your medical condition. This typically includes:

- Medical records from doctors, hospitals, or other healthcare providers that detail your diagnosis, treatment, and prognosis.

- Laboratory and test results, such as X-rays or MRIs, that support your medical condition.

- Statements from healthcare providers outlining how your condition affects your ability to work.

Providing comprehensive medical documentation is crucial to supporting your disability claim and increasing the likelihood of approval.

Additional Information

In addition to the documents mentioned above, you may also need to provide additional information depending on your specific circumstances. This could include:

- Marriage certificates or divorce decrees (for spousal or survivor benefits).

- Adoption or guardianship papers (for dependent benefits).

- Any other relevant documentation requested by the SSA to verify your eligibility or support your claim.

It's important to gather all necessary documentation and information before you begin the application process to ensure a smooth and efficient experience. If you're unsure about what documents you need or how to obtain them, don't hesitate to reach out to a Social Security advisor for guidance and assistance.

With the right documentation in hand, you'll be well-equipped to navigate the application process and access the Social Security benefits you're entitled to receive. So, roll up your sleeves, gather your paperwork, and let's embark on this important journey together towards financial security and peace of mind.

4. Calculating and Maximizing Benefits

The art of maximizing Social Security benefits – a topic that's as intriguing as it is essential for securing your financial future. But fear not, dear reader, for I am here to guide you through the labyrinth of factors that affect your benefit amounts. Let's delve into the intricacies of Social Security calculations, shall we?

4.1 Factors Affecting Benefit Amounts

Earnings Record and Work Credits

At the heart of Social Security benefit calculations lies your earnings record – a comprehensive history of your earnings throughout your working years. Every dollar you earn and every hour you work contribute to this record, shaping the foundation upon which your future benefits will be built.

But here's the catch – in order to qualify for Social Security benefits, you must earn enough "work credits" based on your total earnings. Work credits are essentially a measure of your work history, with one credit earned for every $1,470 of earnings (as of 2021), up to a maximum of four credits per year.

The more work credits you accumulate, the higher your potential benefit amount. So, it pays to stay gainfully employed and contribute to your Social Security earnings record throughout your career.

Full Retirement Age (FRA)

The elusive Full Retirement Age (FRA) – a milestone that holds the key to unlocking your full Social Security benefits. But what exactly is FRA, and why does it matter?

Your FRA is the age at which you become eligible to receive full Social Security retirement benefits – not a moment sooner, not a moment later. For most individuals, FRA falls somewhere between 66 and 67 years old, depending on your birth year.

But here's the twist – you have the option to start receiving benefits as early as age 62, albeit at a reduced monthly amount. On the flip side, you can delay claiming benefits beyond your FRA, up to age 70, and receive a higher monthly benefit as a result.

So, when it comes to maximizing your Social Security benefits, timing is key. By understanding your FRA and weighing the pros and cons of early versus delayed claiming, you can make informed decisions that optimize your financial future.

Primary Insurance Amount (PIA)

 the Primary Insurance Amount (PIA) – the magic number that determines the baseline of your Social Security benefits. But what exactly is PIA, and how is it calculated?

Your PIA represents the monthly benefit amount you are entitled to receive if you claim benefits at your Full Retirement Age (FRA). It's based on your average indexed monthly earnings (AIME) – a weighted average of your highest-earning years adjusted for inflation.

But here's the kicker – your PIA isn't set in stone. It can be adjusted based on various factors, including your claiming age and earnings history. By understanding how your PIA is calculated and how it can be influenced by your claiming decisions, you can take proactive steps to maximize your Social Security benefits and secure your financial future.

Intrigued? I certainly hope so! The world of Social Security benefit calculations is a fascinating and complex landscape, filled with twists, turns, and opportunities for optimization. So, whether you're planning for retirement or navigating the nuances of Social Security disability benefits, remember – knowledge is power. By understanding the factors that affect your benefit amounts, you can chart a course towards a brighter, more secure future.

4.2 Strategies for Maximizing Benefits

the art of maximizing Social Security benefits – a topic that's as fascinating as it is crucial for ensuring a comfortable retirement. Let's delve into some savvy strategies that can help you make the most of this invaluable program:

Delayed Retirement Credits

Picture this: you've reached your full retirement age, but instead of claiming your Social Security benefits right away, you decide to hold off for a few more years. Sound crazy? Not at all! In fact, delaying your Social Security benefits can actually work in your favor – thanks to a little something called delayed retirement credits.

For each year that you delay claiming Social Security benefits beyond your full retirement age, you'll earn a bonus in the form of delayed retirement credits. These credits can increase your monthly benefit amount by as much as 8% per year, up until age 70. So, by delaying your benefits, you not only give yourself more time to save and plan for retirement but also boost your future monthly income in the process. Now, that's what I call a win-win!

Spousal Benefit Optimization

love and marriage – they say it's all about compromise, right? Well, when it comes to Social Security benefits, compromise can actually lead to significant financial gains for both you and your spouse. Enter spousal benefit optimization – a savvy strategy that allows married couples to maximize their Social Security benefits by coordinating their claiming strategies.

Here's how it works: if you're married and your spouse is eligible for Social Security benefits, you may have the option to claim spousal benefits based on their earnings record. By doing so, you can potentially receive a higher benefit amount than if you claimed benefits based on your own earnings history. And the best part? Your spouse's benefits won't be affected by your decision to claim spousal benefits – it's a win-win for both of you!

Claiming Strategies for Couples

When it comes to Social Security benefits, timing is everything – especially for couples. Coordinating your claiming strategies with your spouse can make a world of difference in maximizing your benefits and ensuring a secure retirement for both of you.

One popular claiming strategy for couples is known as "file and suspend." Here's how it works: one spouse files for Social Security benefits at full retirement age but immediately suspends their benefits, allowing them to earn delayed retirement credits while still allowing their spouse to claim spousal benefits. This strategy can help maximize the total benefits received by both spouses over the course of their retirement.

Another option for couples is known as "claim now, claim more later." With this strategy, one spouse claims benefits early while the other delays claiming until later, allowing their benefit amount to increase due to delayed retirement credits. This can be particularly advantageous for couples with a significant age difference or disparate earnings histories.

By carefully considering these and other claiming strategies, couples can optimize their Social Security benefits and enjoy a more financially secure retirement together. After all, when it comes to planning for the future, two heads are often better than one!

5. SOCIAL SECURITY AND WORK

the delicate dance between Social Security benefits and employment – a topic that often raises questions and sparks curiosity. How does one navigate the complexities of working while receiving benefits? What are the earnings limits, and how do they impact your benefits? Fear not, dear reader, for I am here to shed light on this intriguing subject.

5.1 Working While Receiving Benefits

First things first – let's address the common misconception that receiving Social Security benefits means bidding farewell to the workforce forever. Quite the contrary! Many individuals continue to work even as they receive Social Security benefits, finding fulfillment, purpose, and yes, even financial security in the realm of employment.

But how does one go about working while receiving benefits? Is it as simple as clocking in and cashing a paycheck? Well, yes and no. While there are no restrictions on working while receiving Social Security retirement benefits once you reach full retirement age, there are certain rules and limitations to consider if you choose to work before reaching full retirement age.

If you opt to work while receiving Social Security retirement or survivor benefits before reaching full retirement age, you may be subject to the earnings limit set by Social Security. This earnings limit changes annually and is based on your age and your earnings from work. If you earn above the earnings limit, Social Security will withhold a portion of your benefits for every dollar earned above the limit. But fear not – these withheld benefits are not lost forever. Instead, they are recalculated and added back into your future benefits once you reach full retirement age.

5.2 Earnings Limits and Impact on Benefits

Now, you might be wondering – what exactly are these earnings limits, and how do they impact my benefits? Allow me to elucidate. For individuals who have not yet reached full retirement age, the earnings limit for 2024 is $19,560 per year. This means that if you earn more than $19,560 from work in a year, Social Security will withhold $1 in benefits for every $2 earned above the limit.

But fear not, dear reader, for there is a silver lining – once you reach full retirement age, there are no earnings limits to worry about! You can work to your heart's content without fear of Social Security withholding your benefits. And remember, any benefits that were withheld due to excess earnings will be recalculated and added back into your future benefits once you reach full retirement age.

But what if you're receiving Social Security disability benefits? Are the rules the same? Well, not quite. While there are still earnings limits for individuals receiving disability benefits, they are slightly different from those for retirement benefits. The rules surrounding working while receiving disability benefits are complex and may vary depending on your specific circumstances. It's always a good idea to consult with a knowledgeable Social Security advisor to ensure that you understand how working may impact your disability benefits.

Note: working while receiving Social Security benefits is not only possible but quite common among many beneficiaries. By understanding the earnings limits and their impact on your benefits, you can make informed decisions about your employment and financial future. So, whether you're embarking on a new career path or easing into retirement with a part-time gig, rest assured that Social Security benefits are here to support you every step of the way.   5.3 Retirement Earnings Test

5.4 Returning to Work After Retirement

the allure of retirement – the promise of leisurely days, newfound freedom, and the sweet embrace of relaxation. But what happens when the siren call of the workplace beckons once more, drawing retirees back into the fold of employment? Can you return to work after retirement and still receive Social Security benefits? Let's unravel this intriguing conundrum together.

Exploring the Landscape of Retirement and Work

Retirement is often viewed as the culmination of a lifetime of hard work, a well-deserved respite from the daily grind. Many individuals eagerly anticipate the day when they can bid farewell to the office and embrace a slower pace of life. And yet, for some retirees, the allure of the workplace remains strong – whether it's the sense of purpose that comes with a fulfilling career or the desire to supplement retirement income.

But returning to work after retirement raises a host of questions, particularly when it comes to Social Security benefits. Can you continue to receive benefits while working? Will your earnings impact the amount of your benefits? And what are the implications for your retirement strategy?

Understanding the Rules and Regulations

The good news is that, yes, you can indeed return to work after retirement and still receive Social Security benefits. However, there are some important rules and regulations to keep in mind.

First and foremost, your age and your earnings will play a significant role in determining how your benefits are affected. If you have reached full retirement age (which varies depending on your birth year), you can work and earn as much as you'd like without seeing a reduction in your Social Security benefits. That's right – no penalties, no reductions, just the full amount of your hard-earned benefits, no strings attached.

But what if you haven't yet reached full retirement age? here's where things get a bit more complex. If you return to work before reaching full retirement age and earn above a certain threshold, your Social Security benefits may be temporarily reduced. Fear not, though – these reductions are only temporary, and once you reach full retirement age, your benefits will be recalculated to account for the months in which they were reduced.

Maximizing Your Benefits

So, how can you make the most of your Social Security benefits if you decide to return to work after retirement? It's all about strategic planning and understanding the rules of the game.

One key strategy is to carefully consider the timing of your return to work. By waiting until you've reached full retirement age, you can continue to receive your full Social Security benefits regardless of how much you earn. This can be particularly advantageous if you're able to delay claiming benefits until full retirement age, as doing so can result in higher monthly payments.

Another strategy is to explore alternative sources of income during your transition back to work. From part-time employment to freelance gigs to passive income streams, there are myriad ways to supplement your retirement income without jeopardizing your Social Security benefits. By diversifying your income sources, you can mitigate the impact of any temporary reductions in your benefits and ensure a more stable financial future.

Embracing the Journey

Returning to work after retirement is not just about earning a paycheck – it's about embracing new opportunities, pursuing your passions, and finding fulfillment in the work you do. And with Social Security benefits by your side, you can navigate this journey with confidence and peace of mind, knowing that your financial security is safeguarded every step of the way. So, whether you're embarking on a new career path, launching a second act, or simply dipping your toes back into the workforce, remember – the road ahead is yours to explore, and Social Security benefits are here to support you on your journey.

6. Medicare and Social Security

the dynamic duo of retirement benefits – Social Security and Medicare. Together, these two programs form a formidable force, providing comprehensive support to millions of Americans as they navigate the waters of aging and healthcare. But what exactly is Medicare, and how does it coordinate with Social Security benefits? Let's unravel this intricate tapestry together, shall we?

6.1 Introduction to Medicare

First, let's set the stage with a brief introduction to Medicare. Picture this: you've reached the golden age of retirement, basking in the glow of your hard-earned freedom. But along with the joys of retirement come the inevitable realities of aging – including the need for healthcare. That's where Medicare comes into play.

Medicare is a federal health insurance program primarily designed for individuals aged 65 and older. It provides coverage for a wide range of healthcare services, including hospital stays, doctor visits, preventive care, prescription drugs, and more. In essence, Medicare serves as a safety net, offering peace of mind and financial protection against the rising costs of medical care.

But here's the beauty of Medicare – it's not just for seniors. Individuals under the age of 65 with certain disabilities or medical conditions may also qualify for Medicare benefits. This includes individuals with end-stage renal disease (ESRD) or amyotrophic lateral sclerosis (ALS), as well as those receiving Social Security Disability Insurance (SSDI) benefits for a qualifying disability.

6.2 Coordination of Social Security and Medicare Benefits

Now, let's explore how Social Security and Medicare benefits coordinate to provide comprehensive support to eligible individuals.

First and foremost, it's important to understand that while Social Security and Medicare are separate programs, they are closely intertwined. In fact, many individuals become eligible for Medicare benefits automatically when they become eligible for Social Security retirement benefits at age 65.

But here's where things get interesting – the coordination of benefits between Social Security and Medicare can sometimes be a bit...well, complicated. You see, while Medicare provides coverage for healthcare services, Social Security benefits provide financial support for living expenses. So, when it comes to coordinating the two programs, it's crucial to understand how they complement each other.

For example, individuals who receive Social Security retirement benefits may have their Medicare premiums automatically deducted from their Social Security checks. This streamlined process helps ensure that beneficiaries have access to the healthcare coverage they need without the hassle of separate billing.

But wait, there's more! Social Security beneficiaries may also be eligible for assistance with certain Medicare costs through programs like Extra Help and Medicare Savings Programs. These programs help cover expenses such as premiums, deductibles, and copayments, making healthcare more affordable for those on limited incomes.

In essence, the coordination of Social Security and Medicare benefits is like a well-choreographed dance – each program playing its part to ensure that beneficiaries have access to the care and support they need to thrive in their golden years. So, whether you're tapping into your Social Security retirement benefits or navigating the maze of Medicare enrollment, rest assured – you're not alone on this journey. Social Security and Medicare are here to support you every step of the way, ensuring that your retirement years are filled with health, happiness, and peace of mind.   6.3 Enrollment Process and Timing

6.4 Understanding Medicare Coverage Options

the world of healthcare – a labyrinth of terms, options, and decisions that can leave even the savviest of individuals feeling bewildered and overwhelmed. But fear not, dear reader, for I am here to guide you through the intricate landscape of Medicare coverage options with clarity and confidence.

Demystifying Medicare

Before we dive into the nitty-gritty of coverage options, let's take a moment to understand what Medicare is all about. Medicare is a federal health insurance program primarily designed for individuals aged 65 and older, as well as certain younger people with disabilities and those with end-stage renal disease.

Now, Medicare is divided into several parts, each covering different aspects of healthcare services. These parts include:

1. **Medicare Part A**: Often referred to as hospital insurance, Part A helps cover inpatient hospital stays, skilled nursing

facility care, hospice care, and some home health care services.

2. Medicare Part B: Also known as medical insurance, Part B helps cover medically necessary services like doctor's visits, outpatient care, preventive services, and durable medical equipment.

3. Medicare Part C (Medicare Advantage): Offered by private insurance companies approved by Medicare, Part C combines the benefits of Parts A and B, and often includes prescription drug coverage (Part D) as well as additional benefits like dental, vision, and hearing coverage.

4. Medicare Part D: This part provides prescription drug coverage, helping to offset the cost of medications prescribed by healthcare providers.

Now that we have a basic understanding of the different parts of Medicare, let's explore the coverage options available within these parts in more detail.

Exploring Coverage Options

Original Medicare (Parts A and B)

Original Medicare, comprised of Parts A and B, offers comprehensive coverage for hospital and medical services. Part A covers inpatient hospital care, skilled nursing facility care, hospice care, and some home health care services. Part B covers outpatient care, doctor's visits, preventive services, and durable medical equipment.

While Original Medicare provides broad coverage, it does not cover all healthcare costs. Beneficiaries are responsible for paying premiums, deductibles, coinsurance, and copayments. To help offset these costs, many beneficiaries choose to enroll in additional coverage options, such as Medicare Advantage plans or Medicare Supplement Insurance (Medigap) policies.

Medicare Advantage (Part C)

Medicare Advantage plans, offered by private insurance companies approved by Medicare, provide an alternative way to receive Medicare benefits. These plans often include coverage for hospital and medical services, as well as prescription drug coverage (Part D) and additional benefits like dental, vision, and hearing coverage.

Medicare Advantage plans typically have network restrictions and may require beneficiaries to use healthcare providers within the plan's network. However, they may offer lower out-of-pocket costs and additional benefits not covered by Original Medicare.

Medicare Prescription Drug Coverage (Part D)

Medicare Part D provides coverage for prescription drugs, helping beneficiaries afford the cost of medications prescribed by their healthcare providers. Part D plans are offered by private insurance companies approved by Medicare and vary in terms of covered medications, cost-sharing requirements, and monthly premiums.

Beneficiaries can choose a standalone Part D plan to complement Original Medicare or select a Medicare Advantage plan that includes prescription drug coverage as part of its benefits package.

Conclusion

In conclusion, understanding Medicare coverage options is essential for making informed decisions about healthcare coverage in retirement. Whether you opt for Original Medicare with or without additional coverage options, or choose a Medicare Advantage plan for comprehensive benefits, exploring your options and understanding your coverage is key to ensuring access to the healthcare services you need, when you need them. So, take the time to explore your options, ask questions, and make decisions that align with your healthcare needs and preferences. After all, your health and well-being are worth it.

7. Social Security Disability Insurance (SSDI)

Social Security Disability Insurance (SSDI) – a beacon of hope for individuals facing the daunting challenges of disability. Let's embark on a journey to explore the depths of this invaluable program and uncover the vital support it offers to those in need.

7.1 Overview of SSDI Program

Imagine, if you will, a world where a sudden illness or injury leaves you unable to work. Your once-stable livelihood is now in jeopardy, and uncertainty looms large on the horizon. In times like these, SSDI emerges as a lifeline, offering financial assistance to individuals who find themselves unable to engage in substantial gainful activity (SGA) due to a qualifying disability.

But what exactly is SSDI, and how does it work? Well, dear reader, let me shed some light on this essential program.

At its core, SSDI is a federally-funded program administered by the Social Security Administration (SSA). It provides monthly benefits to individuals who have a severe medical condition that prevents them from working and is expected to last for at least one year or result in death.

But here's the thing — qualifying for SSDI benefits isn't as simple as just saying you're disabled. Oh no, my friend, it's a bit more complex than that. To be eligible for SSDI benefits, you must meet a strict set of criteria laid out by the SSA.

First and foremost, you must have worked and paid Social Security taxes for a certain period of time to earn "work credits." These work credits are essentially a measure of your employment history and are based on your total wages or self-employment income. The number of work credits you need to qualify for SSDI benefits depends on your age at the time you become disabled.

Next, you must meet the SSA's definition of disability. Now, this isn't just any old definition — it's a stringent set of criteria designed to ensure that only individuals with severe impairments receive benefits. According to the SSA, you must be unable to perform any substantial gainful activity (SGA) due to your medical condition, and your condition must be expected to last for at least one year or result in death.

But what exactly counts as a qualifying disability, you ask? now that's the million-dollar question. The SSA maintains a comprehensive list of medical conditions that are considered disabling, known as the "Blue Book." This list covers a wide range of impairments, from musculoskeletal disorders to mental disorders to immune system disorders and beyond.

However, even if your condition isn't listed in the Blue Book, fear not! You may still be eligible for SSDI benefits if you can demonstrate that your condition is medically equivalent to one of the listed impairments or if it prevents you from performing any work that you've done in the past or adjusting to other work due to your limitations.

Once you've met the eligibility criteria and submitted your application for SSDI benefits, the SSA will review your case to determine if you qualify for benefits. This process can be lengthy and complex, involving medical evaluations, documentation of your disability, and assessments of your ability to work.

But here's the good news – if your application is approved, you'll receive monthly SSDI payments to help cover living expenses and medical costs. These payments are based on your average lifetime earnings before you became disabled, with higher earners receiving higher benefits.

And perhaps the best part? SSDI benefits also come with access to Medicare – the federal health insurance program for individuals aged 65 and older, as well as those with certain disabilities. This invaluable benefit provides coverage for a wide range of medical services, including doctor visits, hospital stays, prescription drugs, and more.

In summary, SSDI is a vital program that offers crucial financial assistance to individuals facing the challenges of disability. By providing monthly benefits and access to healthcare coverage, SSDI helps ensure that disabled individuals can maintain their dignity and independence in the face of adversity. So, if you or someone you know is struggling with a qualifying disability, don't hesitate to explore the options available through SSDI. After all, in times of need, a helping hand can make all the difference in the world.

7.2 Eligibility Criteria for SSDI Benefits

the world of Social Security Disability Insurance (SSDI) benefits – a lifeline for individuals facing the challenges of a qualifying disability. But who exactly is eligible to receive these crucial benefits? Let's delve into the eligibility criteria to shed some light on this important question.

Eligibility Criteria for SSDI Benefits:

To qualify for SSDI benefits, individuals must meet several key eligibility criteria, as determined by the Social Security Administration (SSA). These criteria are designed to ensure that benefits are provided to those who truly need them, based on their inability to engage in substantial gainful activity

(SGA) due to a disabling condition. Here's a closer look at the eligibility requirements:

1. Medical Condition: The first and most critical criterion for SSDI eligibility is having a qualifying medical condition that meets the SSA's definition of disability. This condition must be expected to last for at least one year or result in death, and it must prevent the individual from performing substantial gainful activity (SGA) – that is, earning a certain amount of income from work.

2. Work Credits: In addition to having a qualifying medical condition, individuals must also have earned a sufficient number of work credits to be eligible for SSDI benefits. Work credits are based on the individual's work history and the amount of Social Security taxes they have paid into the system. The exact number of work credits required depends on the individual's age at the time they became disabled, but most adults need between 20 and 40 credits to qualify.

3. Recent Work: To be eligible for SSDI benefits, individuals must have worked recently enough and for a long enough period to have earned the required number of work credits. The SSA uses a formula called the "recent work test" to determine whether an individual's work history meets the criteria for SSDI eligibility.

4. Severity of Disability: The SSA evaluates the severity of an individual's disability based on their medical records, treatment history, and other evidence provided as part of the application process. The disability must be severe enough to prevent the individual from performing any substantial gainful activity (SGA) – that is, earning a certain amount of income from work – for at least 12 months.

5. Age: While there is no minimum age requirement for SSDI benefits, individuals must be at least 18 years old to qualify. There are also special rules for individuals who became disabled before turning 22, known as "child's benefits," which allow them to qualify for benefits based on a parent's work record.

Meeting these eligibility criteria is crucial for individuals seeking SSDI benefits. It's important to provide thorough documentation of your medical condition, work history, and other relevant information to support your application and demonstrate your eligibility for benefits. If you're unsure whether you meet the criteria for SSDI benefits, consulting with a qualified Social Security advisor can help clarify your situation and guide you through the application process.

7.3 Application Process for SSDI

Now that we've explored the eligibility criteria for SSDI benefits, let's turn our attention to the application process –

the gateway to accessing these crucial financial resources. Navigating the SSDI application process can be complex and daunting, but fear not – I'm here to guide you through each step with clarity and confidence.

Application Process for SSDI:

1. Gather Documentation: Before you begin the application process, it's essential to gather all the necessary documentation to support your claim. This includes medical records, treatment history, work history, and any other relevant information related to your disability.

2. Complete the Application: The first step in applying for SSDI benefits is completing the online application form on the Social Security Administration's website. You can also apply by phone or in person at your local Social Security office if you prefer.

3. Provide Detailed Information: As you complete the application, be sure to provide detailed information about your medical condition, work history, and other relevant factors. The more information you provide, the better equipped the SSA will be to evaluate your claim and determine your eligibility for benefits.

4. Submit Supporting Evidence: Along with your application, you'll need to submit supporting evidence to substantiate your claim of disability. This may include medical records, test results, treatment plans, and statements from healthcare providers documenting the severity of your condition and its impact on your ability to work.

5. Attend Medical Examinations: In some cases, the SSA may require you to undergo medical examinations or evaluations to assess the severity of your disability and determine your eligibility for benefits. It's important to cooperate fully with these examinations and provide any additional information requested by the SSA.

6. Wait for a Decision: After you submit your application and supporting evidence, the SSA will review your claim and make a decision on your eligibility for SSDI benefits. This process can take several months, so it's important to be patient and stay informed about the status of your application.

7. Appeal if Necessary: If your initial application for SSDI benefits is denied, don't lose hope – you have the right to appeal the decision and request a reconsideration of your claim. The appeals process can be complex, but with the help of a qualified Social Security advisor, you can navigate it successfully and advocate for your rights.

By following these steps and staying informed about the SSDI application process, you can maximize your chances of successfully obtaining the benefits you need to support yourself and your family in the face of a qualifying disability. Remember, you're not alone on this journey – I'm here to support you every step of the way.

* * *

8. Supplemental Security Income (SSI)

Supplemental Security Income, often abbreviated as SSI – a lesser-known but equally vital component of the Social Security program. So, what exactly is SSI, and who qualifies for this valuable form of assistance? Let's unravel the mysteries of SSI together.

8.1 What is SSI and Who Qualifies?

Supplemental Security Income, or SSI, is a federal income assistance program designed to provide financial support to elderly, blind, or disabled individuals with limited income and resources. Unlike Social Security benefits, which are based on an individual's work history and earnings, SSI is a needs-based program, meaning eligibility is determined by financial need rather than work credits.

But what does this mean in practical terms? Well, it means that SSI serves as a lifeline for individuals who may not have a significant work history or who may be unable to work due to a disability. Whether you're a senior struggling to make ends meet on a fixed income, a blind individual navigating the challenges of daily life, or a person with a disability facing financial hardship, SSI may offer the support you need to maintain a basic standard of living.

Now, you might be wondering, "Who exactly qualifies for SSI benefits?" an excellent question indeed. Let's delve into the eligibility criteria and shed some light on this important topic.

Who Qualifies for SSI?

To qualify for Supplemental Security Income, individuals must meet certain eligibility requirements established by the Social Security Administration (SSA). These requirements typically revolve around three main factors: age, disability status, and financial need.

1. Age: Individuals must be aged 65 or older to qualify for SSI based on age alone. However, individuals under the age of 65 may also qualify if they meet the criteria for blindness or disability.

2. Disability Status: Individuals under the age of 65 may qualify for SSI if they have a qualifying disability that prevents them from engaging in substantial gainful activity (SGA) and is expected to last for at least one year or result in death. The SSA uses a strict definition of disability when evaluating SSI claims, considering both the severity of the impairment and its impact on the individual's ability to work.

3. Financial Need: Perhaps the most crucial aspect of SSI eligibility is financial need. To qualify for SSI, individuals must have limited income and resources, as determined by the SSA. Income includes wages, Social Security benefits, pensions, and any other form of financial support, while resources encompass assets such as bank accounts, stocks, and real estate. The SSA sets specific income and resource limits each year, and individuals must fall below these limits to qualify for SSI.

In addition to these basic eligibility criteria, certain groups of individuals may receive expedited or simplified processing of their SSI claims. This includes individuals who are blind, individuals residing in institutions, and certain children with disabilities.

In summary, Supplemental Security Income (SSI) is a critical lifeline for individuals with limited income and resources who are elderly, blind, or disabled. By providing financial support to those in need, SSI helps ensure that no one falls through the cracks in our social safety net. So, if you or someone you know meets the eligibility criteria for SSI, don't hesitate to explore this valuable form of assistance. After all, everyone deserves the opportunity to live with dignity and security, regardless of their circumstances.

8.2 Eligibility Criteria for SSI Benefits

Supplemental Security Income (SSI) benefits – a lifeline for those facing financial hardship and in need of extra support. But who exactly is eligible to receive these vital benefits? Let's dive into the eligibility criteria and uncover the path to accessing SSI benefits.

Eligibility Criteria for SSI Benefits:

To qualify for SSI benefits, individuals must meet certain criteria related to their income, resources, and citizenship or residency status. Let's break down these criteria in more detail:

1. Income Requirements: SSI benefits are intended for individuals with limited income and resources. To be eligible, your countable income must fall below the federal benefit rate (FBR), which is the maximum monthly benefit amount set by the Social Security Administration (SSA). Countable income includes wages, Social Security benefits, pensions, and other sources of income, but certain exclusions may apply.

2. Resource Limits: In addition to income, individuals must also meet resource limits to qualify for SSI benefits. Resources include cash, bank accounts, stocks, bonds, and other assets that could be converted into cash and used for food or shelter. The resource limit for individuals is typically $2,000, while couples may have up to $3,000 in countable resources.

3. Citizenship or Residency Status: To receive SSI benefits, you must be either a U.S. citizen or a qualified non-citizen who meets certain criteria. Qualified non-citizens include lawful permanent residents, refugees, asylees, and certain other immigrants with permission to live and work in the United States. Non-citizens must also meet additional eligibility requirements related to their immigration status.

4. Disability or Age: While SSI benefits are primarily intended for individuals with disabilities, certain aged individuals (65 years old or older) who meet the income and resource requirements may also qualify for benefits. To be considered disabled for SSI purposes, you must have a physical or mental impairment that prevents you from engaging in substantial gainful activity and is expected to last for at least 12 months or result in death.

5. Medical Evidence: When applying for SSI benefits based on disability, you will need to provide medical evidence to support your claim. This may include medical records, test results, treatment history, and statements from healthcare providers detailing the nature and severity of your impairment.

Meeting these eligibility criteria is crucial for individuals seeking to access SSI benefits and receive the financial assistance they need to meet their basic needs. But once you've determined that you meet the eligibility requirements, the next step is to navigate the application process.

8.3 Applying for SSI Benefits

Applying for SSI benefits may seem daunting at first, but fear not – the Social Security Administration (SSA) is here to guide you through the process. Let's explore the steps involved in applying for SSI benefits and how you can maximize your chances of success.

1. Gather Necessary Documents:

Before you begin the application process, gather any documents and information you'll need to complete your application. This may include:

- Social Security number

- Proof of age

- Proof of citizenship or immigration status

- Bank statements and other financial records

- Medical records and documentation of your disability

Having these documents on hand will streamline the application process and ensure that you have all the information you need to complete your application accurately.

2. Submit Your Application:

There are several ways to apply for SSI benefits:

- **Online:** You can apply for SSI benefits online through the SSA's website using the Adult Disability Report (ADR) or the SSI Application.

- **By Phone:** You can call the SSA's toll-free number and schedule an appointment to apply for benefits over the phone.

- **In Person:** If you prefer, you can visit your local Social Security office in person to complete your application with the assistance of a representative.

Choose the method that works best for you and submit your application along with any required documentation.

3. Attend Disability Interviews:

If you're applying for SSI benefits based on disability, you may be required to attend one or more interviews with SSA representatives. These interviews are an opportunity for you to provide additional information about your disability and medical history, as well as to ask any questions you may have about the application process.

4. Follow Up on Your Application:

Once you've submitted your application, be sure to follow up with the SSA to check on its status. You can do this by logging into your my Social Security account online, calling the SSA's toll-free number, or visiting your local Social Security office.

5. Provide Additional Information:

During the application process, the SSA may request additional information or documentation to support your claim for SSI benefits. Be sure to respond promptly to any requests for information to avoid delays in processing your application.

By following these steps and staying informed about the application process, you can increase your chances of successfully applying for SSI benefits and accessing the financial assistance you need to support yourself and your family. Remember, the SSA is here to help you every step of the way – so don't hesitate to reach out if you have any questions or need assistance with your application.

9. Common Questions and Myths

the realm of Social Security – shrouded in mystery, rife with misconceptions, and brimming with questions waiting to be answered. As a seasoned Social Security advisor, I've heard them all – from the practical to the perplexing, the mundane to the mind-boggling. So, without further ado, let's dive into some of the most frequently asked questions (FAQs) about Social Security:

9.1 Frequently Asked Questions (FAQs)

Q: When should I apply for Social Security benefits?

A: the age-old question – quite literally! The ideal age to apply for Social Security benefits depends on a variety of factors, including your individual circumstances, financial needs, and health status. While you can start receiving benefits as early as age 62, doing so may result in a reduced monthly benefit. On the other hand, delaying retirement can lead to higher benefit amounts. Ultimately, the decision boils down to your unique situation and goals.

Q: How are Social Security benefits calculated?

A: the million-dollar question – or should I say, the Social Security benefits question! Your Social Security benefits are calculated based on your average lifetime earnings, also known as your "primary insurance amount" (PIA). The Social Security Administration (SSA) considers your highest 35 years of earnings, adjusts them for inflation, and applies a formula to determine your benefit amount. Understanding this calculation can help you make informed decisions about when to claim benefits and how to maximize your Social Security income.

Q: Can I work while receiving Social Security benefits?

A: the age-old dilemma – work or retire? The short answer is yes, you can work while receiving Social Security benefits. However, there are limits on how much you can earn before your benefits are reduced, known as the "earnings limit." If you earn above this limit, your benefits may be temporarily reduced until you reach full retirement age. Once you reach full retirement age, you can work and earn as much as you'd like without any impact on your benefits.

Q: Will Social Security be there for me when I retire?

A: the existential question of our time – will Social Security survive? Rest assured, dear reader, Social Security is here to stay. While concerns about the program's long-term solvency are valid, the reality is that Social Security benefits are funded through payroll taxes and backed by the full faith and credit of the United States government. With careful planning and prudent policymaking, Social Security will continue to provide vital support to retirees for generations to come.

Q: Can I receive Social Security benefits if I've never worked?

A: the misconception that plagues many – Social Security benefits are not just for retirees with a lengthy work history. In fact, certain family members of eligible workers may also qualify for benefits based on the worker's earnings record. Spouses, children, and even dependent parents may be eligible for benefits, provided they meet the criteria set forth by the Social Security Administration. So, even if you've never worked a day in your life, you may still be entitled to Social Security benefits through a qualifying relationship with a beneficiary.

Q: What happens if I change my mind about claiming Social Security benefits?

A: the freedom to change course – it's a beautiful thing! If you've already started receiving Social Security benefits but have a change of heart, fear not. The SSA allows beneficiaries to withdraw their application for benefits within the first 12 months of receiving them. However, keep in mind that you'll be required to repay any benefits you've already received, and you can only withdraw your application once in your lifetime. So, if you're contemplating a change of plans, be sure to weigh the pros and cons carefully before making a decision.

 the world of Social Security – a labyrinth of rules, regulations, and, yes, frequently asked questions. But fear not, dear reader, for armed with knowledge and guidance, you can navigate this complex terrain with confidence and clarity. And remember, when in doubt, don't hesitate to reach out to a qualified Social Security advisor for assistance. After all, we're here to help unravel the mysteries of Social Security and empower you to make informed decisions about your financial future.

9.2 Dispelling Common Myths about Social Security

 myths – those pesky little whispers of misinformation that can cloud our judgment and lead us astray. When it comes to Social Security, there are plenty of myths swirling around, casting doubt on the integrity and effectiveness of this vital program. But fear not, dear reader, for I am here to shine a light on these misconceptions and set the record straight once and for all.

Myth 1: Social Security is Going Broke

the age-old myth that Social Security is teetering on the brink of insolvency, destined to collapse under the weight of its own obligations. But here's the truth: Social Security is far from bankrupt. While it's true that the program faces long-term funding challenges due to factors such as an aging population and declining birth rates, it's important to remember that Social Security has weathered similar storms in the past. With prudent reforms and responsible fiscal management, Social Security can remain solvent for generations to come.

Myth 2: Social Security is Only for Retirees

retirement – the quintessential image of Social Security benefits. But here's the thing: Social Security is not just for retirees. In fact, the program provides crucial support to individuals with disabilities, survivors of deceased workers, and certain family members of eligible beneficiaries. Whether you're coping with a debilitating medical condition, grieving the loss of a loved one, or supporting a family member in need, Social Security benefits may offer you a lifeline in times of hardship.

Myth 3: Social Security Benefits are Generous

the misconception that Social Security benefits provide a lavish lifestyle akin to a tropical paradise. But here's the reality check: Social Security benefits are designed to provide a basic level of financial support, not to fund a life of luxury. The average monthly benefit amount is modest, and for many recipients, it's not enough to cover all their living expenses. Social Security is meant to supplement other sources of income, such as pensions, savings, and investments, not to replace them entirely.

Myth 4: Social Security is a Ponzi Scheme

the comparison to a notorious financial scam that evokes images of deceit and deception. But here's the truth: Social Security is not a Ponzi scheme. Unlike a Ponzi scheme, which relies on new investors to pay returns to earlier investors, Social Security operates as a pay-as-you-go system, with current workers paying taxes to support current beneficiaries. While the program does face long-term funding challenges, it is fundamentally different from a Ponzi scheme and has a solid foundation of public trust and government backing.

Myth 5: Social Security is Welfare

the misconception that Social Security benefits are akin to handouts from the government, reserved only for the needy and deserving. But here's the reality: Social Security is not welfare. It's an earned benefit – a return on the contributions that workers have made throughout their careers through payroll taxes. Whether you're a high-earning executive or a blue-collar worker, Social Security benefits are yours by right, based on your years of hard work and dedication to the workforce.

Myth 6: Social Security is Optional

the misconception that participation in Social Security is optional, leaving individuals free to opt out of the program if they so choose. But here's the reality: for the vast majority of American workers, participation in Social Security is mandatory. Most employees are required to pay Social Security taxes on their earnings, with the taxes automatically deducted from their paychecks. These contributions fund the Social Security system and entitle workers to future benefits based on their earnings history.

Myth 7: Social Security Benefits are Tax-Free

The belief that Social Security benefits are exempt from taxation, allowing recipients to enjoy their retirement income without the burden of additional taxes. But here's the truth: while Social Security benefits are not subject to federal income tax for some individuals, they may be taxable for others. The taxability of Social Security benefits depends on your total income and filing status. If your combined income exceeds certain thresholds, a portion of your Social Security benefits may be subject to federal income tax.

Myth 8: Social Security Benefits Will Be Enough to Retire Comfortably

the misconception that Social Security benefits alone will provide enough income to sustain a comfortable retirement lifestyle, allowing retirees to kick back and enjoy their golden years without a care in the world. But here's the reality: for many Americans, Social Security benefits are just one piece of the retirement income puzzle. While they can provide valuable support, especially for lower-income retirees, they are unlikely to fully replace pre-retirement income or cover all living expenses. It's essential for individuals to supplement their Social Security benefits with other sources of retirement income, such as pensions, savings, and investments, in order to achieve a financially secure retirement.

Myth 9: Social Security Benefits Will Be Available Forever

the belief that Social Security benefits will be available indefinitely, providing a reliable source of income for generations to come. But here's the sobering truth: without reforms to address its long-term funding challenges, Social Security may face cuts to benefits or changes to eligibility criteria in the future. While the program is currently solvent and able to pay full benefits for the foreseeable future, demographic shifts such as an aging population and declining birth rates pose significant challenges to its sustainability. It's essential for policymakers to take action to shore up Social Security's finances and ensure its viability for future generations.

Myth 10: Social Security Is Only for Those Who Haven't Saved Enough

the misconception that Social Security benefits are reserved only for those who have failed to save enough for retirement, serving as a safety net for the financially irresponsible. But here's the reality: Social Security benefits are available to all eligible workers, regardless of their savings or financial planning efforts. Whether you've diligently saved for retirement or faced unforeseen financial challenges along the way, Social Security benefits are yours by right, based on your contributions to the system throughout your working years.

Myth 11: Social Security Benefits Can Be Garnished for Debt Repayment

the misconception that Social Security benefits are fair game for creditors and debt collectors, allowing them to garnish these vital funds to repay outstanding debts. But here's the truth: Social Security benefits are generally protected from garnishment by most creditors. Under federal law, Social

Security benefits are exempt from garnishment for most types of debt, including credit card debt, medical bills, and student loans. This protection ensures that Social Security beneficiaries can rely on their benefits to cover essential living expenses without fear of seizure by creditors.

Myth 12: Social Security Benefits Are Indexed to Inflation

the belief that Social Security benefits automatically increase to keep pace with rising prices and inflation, ensuring that beneficiaries maintain their purchasing power over time. But here's the reality: while Social Security benefits are adjusted annually based on changes in the Consumer Price Index for Urban Wage Earners and Clerical Workers (CPI-W), these cost-of-living adjustments (COLAs) may not fully offset the impact of inflation for all beneficiaries. In recent years, COLAs have often been modest, leading to concerns about the erosion of purchasing power for Social Security recipients, especially as healthcare and housing costs continue to rise.

Myth 13: Social Security Benefits Are Guaranteed

the misconception that Social Security benefits are guaranteed by the government, providing an ironclad assurance of financial security for retirees, individuals with disabilities, and survivors. But here's the sobering truth: while Social Security benefits are backed by the full faith and credit of the U.S. government, there are no guarantees that benefit levels will remain unchanged in the future. Policymakers have the authority to make changes to the Social Security program, including adjustments to benefit amounts, eligibility criteria, and tax rates, in response to shifting economic and demographic trends. While Social Security is considered a stable and reliable source of income, it's essential for beneficiaries to remain vigilant and advocate for policies that protect and strengthen the program for future generations.

Myth 14: Social Security Benefits Are Only Available to Those Who Worked in the Private Sector

the misconception that Social Security benefits are exclusively for individuals who worked in the private sector, leaving out those who served in the public sector or pursued careers in other fields. But here's the reality: Social Security benefits are available to most workers in the United States, regardless of their employment history or sector. While certain government employees may be covered by alternative retirement systems such as the Civil Service Retirement System (CSRS) or the Federal Employees Retirement System (FERS), many public sector workers are also covered by Social Security and may be eligible for benefits based on their earnings from covered employment. Additionally, self-employed individuals and workers in non-traditional employment arrangements may also qualify for Social Security benefits, provided they meet the program's eligibility criteria.

In conclusion, Dear reader, let us not be swayed by the myths and misconceptions that surround Social Security. By seeking out accurate information and understanding the realities of the program, we can ensure that Social Security remains a vital source of support and security for generations to come.

10. SOCIAL SECURITY AND TAXES

Taxes – the inevitable reality of adult life. We're all familiar with the annual ritual of filing our tax returns, navigating a maze of forms and deductions in the hopes of minimizing our financial obligations to the government. But did you know that Social Security benefits can also be subject to taxation? That's right – even in retirement, Uncle Sam still wants his share.

10.1 Taxation of Social Security Benefits

So, how does the taxation of Social Security benefits work, you might ask? Well, it's a bit like playing a game of financial chess – there are rules, strategies, and sometimes, unexpected twists and turns. Let's break it down, shall we?

Understanding the Thresholds:

The first thing to know is that not all Social Security benefits are subject to taxation. Whether or not your benefits are taxed depends on your total income for the year, including your Social Security benefits, as well as any other sources of income you may have, such as pensions, wages, or investment income.

The IRS uses a formula known as the "combined income" or "provisional income" to determine whether your Social Security benefits are taxable. This combined income is calculated by adding up half of your Social Security benefits plus all other sources of income. If your combined income exceeds certain thresholds, a portion of your Social Security benefits may be subject to taxation.

Determining the Taxable Portion:

Once your combined income exceeds the applicable threshold, the next step is to determine the percentage of your Social Security benefits that are taxable. The IRS uses a sliding scale to calculate this percentage, based on your filing status and income level.

For example, if you're a single filer with a combined income between $25,000 and $34,000, up to 50% of your Social Security benefits may be subject to taxation. If your combined income exceeds $34,000, up to 85% of your benefits may be taxable. The thresholds are slightly higher for married couples filing jointly.

Strategies to Minimize Taxes:

Now, here's where things get interesting – there are strategies you can employ to minimize the amount of taxes you owe on your Social Security benefits. One common tactic is to carefully manage the timing of withdrawals from retirement accounts and other sources of income. By strategically timing your withdrawals, you can minimize your combined income in years when you expect to receive Social Security benefits, thereby reducing your tax liability.

Another strategy is to consider the tax implications of other sources of income, such as Roth IRA withdrawals or capital gains from investments. By diversifying your income streams and taking advantage of tax-advantaged accounts, you can potentially reduce the portion of your Social Security benefits that are subject to taxation.

Stay Informed and Plan Ahead:

As with any aspect of financial planning, staying informed and proactive is key to minimizing your tax burden on Social Security benefits. By understanding the rules and thresholds for taxation, as well as employing smart strategies to manage your income, you can ensure that you keep more of your hard-earned money in your pocket where it belongs.

So, while taxes may not be the most exciting topic of conversation, understanding the taxation of Social Security benefits is an essential part of planning for your financial future in retirement. By arming yourself with knowledge and taking proactive steps to minimize your tax liability, you can make the most of your Social Security benefits and enjoy a more secure and comfortable retirement.

10.2 Reporting Social Security Income on Tax Returns

Certainly! Let's delve into the topic of reporting Social Security income on tax returns with an engaging approach.

10.2 Reporting Social Security Income on Tax Returns

Tax season – a time of year that elicits a collective groan from many Americans. But fear not, dear taxpayer, for navigating the intricacies of tax returns doesn't have to be a daunting task. In fact, reporting Social Security income on your tax return can be as smooth as sailing on a calm sea with a gentle breeze at your back. So, grab your metaphorical sailboat, and let's embark on this journey together!

First things first – what exactly is Social Security income, and why does it matter come tax time? Well, if you're one of the millions of Americans receiving Social Security benefits, you're in luck – you've got income to report! Social Security income includes any payments you receive from the Social Security Administration, whether it's retirement benefits, disability benefits, survivor benefits, or any other type of Social Security payment.

Now, here's where things get interesting – or perhaps slightly less exhilarating, depending on your perspective. The IRS treats Social Security income differently depending on your total income and filing status. For some lucky souls, Social

Security income may be entirely tax-free. For others, a portion of their Social Security benefits may be subject to taxation.

So, how do you determine if your Social Security benefits are taxable? Well, it all comes down to a magical number known as your "combined income." Your combined income is calculated by adding half of your Social Security benefits to all your other income sources, including wages, self-employment income, interest, dividends, and any other taxable income.

Once you've calculated your combined income, it's time to consult the IRS gods – I mean, guidelines – to see if your benefits are taxable. If you're a single filer with a combined income between $25,000 and $34,000, or a joint filer with a combined income between $32,000 and $44,000, up to 50% of your Social Security benefits may be subject to taxation. And if you're really living the high life with a combined income exceeding those thresholds, up to 85% of your benefits could be fair game for the taxman.

But fear not, for there are strategies you can employ to minimize the tax bite on your Social Security benefits. For starters, consider spreading out withdrawals from retirement accounts over multiple years to keep your combined income below the taxable thresholds. Additionally, you may qualify for tax deductions and credits that can help offset the tax burden on your Social Security benefits.

Now, you may be wondering – how exactly do I report my Social Security income on my tax return? Ah, the million-dollar question! (Well, maybe not quite a million dollars, but you get the idea.) Reporting your Social Security income is a relatively straightforward process. You'll receive a Form SSA-1099 from the Social Security Administration detailing the amount of benefits you received during the tax year. Simply take that information and plug it into the appropriate line on your tax return – typically line 6a of Form 1040 or line 14a of Form 1040-SR.

And there you have it – reporting Social Security income on your tax return demystified! So, as you embark on your tax-filing adventure, remember that you're not alone. With a little bit of knowledge and a sprinkle of patience, you'll navigate the seas of taxation with confidence and grace. Fair winds and following seas, dear taxpayer – may your refund be plentiful and your audits be few!

10.3 Strategies for Minimizing Tax Impact

taxes – the unavoidable reality of life. But fear not, savvy savers and diligent planners, for there are strategies aplenty to help minimize the tax impact on your Social Security benefits. Let's dive into some smart tactics to keep more of your hard-earned money in your pocket where it belongs:

1. Manage Your Income Sources Wisely:

One of the most effective ways to minimize taxes on your Social Security benefits is to carefully manage your income sources. By strategically timing withdrawals from retirement accounts, such as traditional IRAs or 401(k)s, you can control your taxable income and potentially reduce the portion of your benefits subject to taxation.

Consider spreading out withdrawals over multiple years or delaying withdrawals until after you start receiving Social Security benefits. This can help keep your combined income below the thresholds at which Social Security benefits become taxable, allowing you to retain more of your benefits tax-free.

2. Invest in Tax-Advantaged Accounts:

Another savvy strategy is to invest in tax-advantaged accounts, such as Roth IRAs or Health Savings Accounts (HSAs). Unlike traditional retirement accounts, withdrawals from Roth IRAs are tax-free, making them an excellent option for minimizing your taxable income in retirement.

Similarly, contributions to HSAs are tax-deductible, and withdrawals for qualified medical expenses are tax-free. By leveraging these tax-advantaged accounts, you can reduce your taxable income and potentially lower the portion of your Social Security benefits subject to taxation.

3. Consider Delaying Social Security Benefits:

While it may be tempting to start collecting Social Security benefits as soon as you're eligible, delaying benefits can actually be a smart tax strategy. By delaying benefits past your full retirement age (up to age 70), you can increase the size of your monthly benefit payments and potentially reduce the percentage of benefits subject to taxation.

Delaying benefits can also allow you to continue working and earning income, which can help offset the tax impact of your Social Security benefits. Plus, for every year you delay benefits past your full retirement age, you'll earn delayed retirement credits, which can boost your benefit amount even further.

4. Coordinate with Your Spouse:

If you're married, coordinating your Social Security claiming strategy with your spouse can help maximize your benefits and minimize taxes. For example, if one spouse has significantly higher lifetime earnings than the other, they may choose to delay benefits to maximize their payout, while the lower-earning spouse claims benefits earlier to provide additional income.

By carefully coordinating your claiming strategy, you can optimize your combined Social Security benefits and minimize the tax impact on your household income. This may involve considering factors such as age differences, life expectancies, and other sources of retirement income.

5. Stay Informed and Seek Professional Advice:

Finally, staying informed about changes to tax laws and seeking professional advice from a financial advisor or tax professional can help ensure that you're making smart decisions to minimize the tax impact on your Social Security benefits. A knowledgeable advisor can help you navigate the complexities of tax planning in retirement and develop a personalized strategy to maximize your benefits and minimize taxes.

In conclusion, while taxes may be a fact of life, they don't have to take a big bite out of your Social Security benefits. By employing smart tax strategies, managing your income sources wisely, and seeking professional advice, you can minimize the tax impact on your benefits and enjoy a more secure and comfortable retirement.

11. Future of Social Security

As we gaze into the crystal ball of the future, it's impossible to ignore the looming challenges that lie ahead for the Social Security program. While Social Security has been a lifeline for millions of Americans since its inception, demographic shifts, economic realities, and political uncertainties threaten to disrupt the stability of the program in the years to come.

11.1 Challenges Facing the Social Security Program

1. Demographic Shifts:

One of the most pressing challenges facing Social Security is the aging population. As the Baby Boomer generation enters retirement in droves, the number of retirees drawing benefits from the program is expected to soar. Meanwhile, the workforce – and thus the number of workers contributing to Social Security through payroll taxes – is growing at a slower pace. This demographic imbalance threatens to strain the financial resources of the program and raise questions about its long-term sustainability.

2. Funding Shortfalls:

In recent years, Social Security has faced mounting concerns about its long-term solvency. The Social Security Trust Fund, which helps finance benefit payments, is projected to be depleted within the next couple of decades if no action is taken to address funding shortfalls. This raises the specter of benefit cuts, tax increases, or other measures to shore up the program's finances – all of which could have significant implications for retirees and future generations.

3. Economic Uncertainty:

The health of the economy also plays a critical role in the future of Social Security. Economic downturns can lead to higher unemployment rates, lower wages, and reduced tax revenues – all of which can strain the financial resources of the program. In addition, longer life expectancies and rising healthcare costs may increase the financial burden on Social Security, further exacerbating funding challenges.

4. Political Gridlock:

As if the demographic and economic challenges weren't enough, Social Security also faces the perennial obstacle of political gridlock. Discussions about potential reforms to strengthen the program – such as raising the retirement age, adjusting benefit formulas, or increasing payroll taxes – often devolve into partisan squabbles and ideological debates. This political stalemate makes it difficult to enact meaningful changes to address the program's long-term sustainability.

5. Changing Social Norms:

Finally, changing social norms and attitudes toward retirement and work may also impact the future of Social Security. With more Americans working longer and pursuing non-traditional career paths, the dynamics of the workforce are shifting in ways that could affect the program's finances and structure. Additionally, evolving family structures and caregiving responsibilities may influence the demand for Social Security benefits and support services in the years to come.

6. Technological Advancements:

In an increasingly digital world, technological advancements present both opportunities and challenges for the Social Security program. While automation and digitalization can streamline administrative processes and improve efficiency, they also raise concerns about data security, privacy, and access to services for individuals who may not be technologically savvy or have reliable internet access.

7. Income Inequality:

Rising income inequality is another factor that may impact the future of Social Security. As wealth becomes increasingly concentrated among the top earners, there may be growing pressure to address disparities in Social Security benefits and contributions. Efforts to address income inequality – such as raising the cap on earnings subject to Social Security taxes or implementing means-testing for benefits – could reshape the program's funding structure and distributional outcomes.

8. Longevity Trends:

Longevity trends present both opportunities and challenges for the Social Security program. On one hand, longer life expectancies mean that retirees may need to rely on Social Security benefits for a longer period of time, increasing the financial strain on the program. On the other hand, longer life expectancies also provide opportunities for individuals to work longer and contribute more to the program, potentially offsetting some of the financial pressures associated with an aging population.

9. Globalization:

In an increasingly interconnected world, globalization has implications for the future of Social Security. International mobility and labor market integration may impact the distribution of Social Security benefits and contributions, particularly for individuals who have worked in multiple countries throughout their careers. Efforts to harmonize Social Security systems across borders and address cross-border issues such as benefit coordination and portability will become increasingly important in the years to come.

10. Climate Change and Environmental Challenges:

While it may seem unrelated at first glance, climate change and environmental challenges can also impact the future of

Social Security. Extreme weather events, natural disasters, and environmental degradation can have profound economic consequences, leading to job losses, property damage, and increased demand for social safety net programs like Social Security. Efforts to mitigate and adapt to climate change will therefore be critical for ensuring the long-term viability of the Social Security program.

In conclusion, the challenges facing the Social Security program are multifaceted and interconnected, encompassing demographic shifts, funding shortfalls, economic uncertainty, political gridlock, technological advancements, income inequality, longevity trends, globalization, and environmental challenges. Addressing these challenges will require proactive and collaborative efforts from policymakers, stakeholders, and the public to ensure that Social Security remains a pillar of financial security and stability for generations to come.

11.3 Ensuring Sustainability for Future Generations

the future – a vast and uncertain landscape, filled with endless possibilities and daunting challenges. As we stand on the precipice of tomorrow, one question looms large: How can we ensure the sustainability of Social Security for future generations?

Understanding the Challenge:

To grasp the enormity of the task ahead, we must first understand the challenges facing Social Security. Demographic shifts, economic fluctuations, and political pressures all threaten to destabilize the delicate balance of the program. As the population ages and life expectancy increases, the strain on Social Security's resources grows ever greater. Meanwhile, economic downturns and changing employment patterns can disrupt the flow of revenue into the program, further exacerbating the problem.

Exploring Solutions:

So, what can be done to address these challenges and secure the future of Social Security for generations to come? The answer lies in a combination of prudent policy reforms, responsible fiscal management, and innovative thinking.

1. Adjusting the Retirement Age:

One potential solution is to gradually increase the full retirement age – the age at which individuals become eligible for full Social Security benefits. By raising the retirement age in line with increases in life expectancy, we can help ensure that the program remains financially sustainable over the long term.

2. Implementing Means Testing:

Means testing – the practice of adjusting benefits based on an individual's income or assets – could also help shore up Social Security's finances. By targeting benefits to those who need them most, we can reduce the strain on the program while ensuring that it continues to provide a safety net for the most vulnerable members of society.

3. Enhancing Revenue Streams:

Another approach is to explore ways to enhance Social Security's revenue streams. This could include increasing payroll taxes, raising the cap on taxable earnings, or implementing new revenue sources such as a dedicated Social Security tax on investment income.

4. Promoting Economic Growth:

Finally, fostering economic growth and increasing productivity can help generate the resources needed to sustain Social Security over the long term. By investing in education, infrastructure, and innovation, we can create a stronger, more resilient economy that benefits all Americans.

Embracing Innovation:

In addition to these traditional approaches, embracing innovation and harnessing the power of technology could also play a crucial role in securing Social Security's future. From streamlining administrative processes to improving data analytics and fraud detection, technology has the potential to make Social Security more efficient, cost-effective, and responsive to the needs of beneficiaries.

Collaborative Efforts:

Ultimately, ensuring the sustainability of Social Security will require a collaborative effort from policymakers, stakeholders, and the public at large. It will require foresight, creativity, and a willingness to make difficult choices in the face of uncertainty. But with determination and resolve, we can rise to the challenge and ensure that Social Security remains a cornerstone of economic security and social justice for generations to come.

As we look ahead to the future, let us remember the words of Franklin D. Roosevelt, the architect of Social Security: "The test of our progress is not whether we add more to the abundance of those who have much; it is whether we provide enough for those who have too little." By working together and staying true to the values that define us as a nation, we can build a brighter, more secure future for all Americans.

12. Resources and Support

Navigating the world of Social Security can feel like embarking on a journey through uncharted territory. With its complex rules, intricate calculations, and ever-changing landscape, it's no wonder that many individuals find themselves feeling overwhelmed and confused. But fear not, dear reader, for you are not alone on this journey. There are resources and support systems in place to help guide you through the maze of Social Security, ensuring that you have the information and assistance you need every step of the way.

12.1 Social Security Administration (SSA) Resources

At the heart of the Social Security universe lies the Social Security Administration (SSA) – the federal agency responsible for administering the program and providing a wealth of resources and support to the public. Whether you're a seasoned retiree, a newly disabled individual, or a grieving survivor, the SSA is your one-stop shop for all things Social Security.

SSA Website:

The SSA's website is a treasure trove of information, offering a vast array of resources, tools, and publications to help you better understand Social Security benefits and services. From detailed explanations of benefit programs to interactive calculators for estimating your retirement benefits, the SSA website has something for everyone.

Online Services:

In today's digital age, convenience is key – and the SSA delivers with its suite of online services. Through the SSA website, you can apply for benefits, check the status of your application, request a replacement Social Security card, and even update your personal information – all from the comfort of your own home.

Publications and Forms:

Need a deeper dive into the intricacies of Social Security? Look no further than the SSA's extensive collection of publications and forms. Whether you're seeking guidance on retirement planning, disability eligibility criteria, or survivor benefits, you'll find a wealth of resources at your fingertips.

Local Social Security Offices:

Sometimes, nothing beats the personal touch of face-to-face interaction. That's where your local Social Security office comes in. With over 1,200 offices nationwide, the SSA has a presence in nearly every community, offering in-person assistance and support to individuals seeking guidance on their Social Security journey.

Toll-Free Helpline:

Got a burning question about Social Security? Don't hesitate to pick up the phone and dial the SSA's toll-free helpline. Staffed by knowledgeable representatives ready to assist you with your inquiries, the helpline is a valuable resource for individuals seeking clarification on benefit eligibility, application procedures, and more.

Outreach and Education:

In addition to its online and in-person resources, the SSA is committed to outreach and education, ensuring that individuals from all walks of life have access to the information they need to make informed decisions about their Social Security benefits. From community workshops to informational seminars, the SSA's outreach efforts are designed to empower individuals with the knowledge and tools they need to secure their financial future.

In conclusion, the Social Security Administration is not just a bureaucratic entity – it's a lifeline for millions of Americans, providing essential resources and support to help navigate the complexities of Social Security with confidence and ease. So whether you're planning for retirement, coping with a disability, or seeking assistance as a survivor, remember that help is always just a click, call, or visit away.

12.2 Online Tools and Calculators

In today's digital age, navigating the intricacies of Social Security benefits has never been easier, thanks to a wealth of online tools and calculators at your fingertips. Whether you're planning for retirement, estimating your disability benefits, or exploring survivor benefits for your loved ones, these online resources can provide valuable insights and guidance to help you make informed decisions about your financial future.

Retirement Estimator:

One of the most popular online tools offered by the Social Security Administration (SSA) is the Retirement Estimator. This handy tool allows you to input your earnings history and projected retirement age to receive an estimate of your future Social Security benefits. By playing around with different retirement scenarios, you can gain valuable insights into how your benefit amount may change based on factors such as your retirement age and earnings history.

Benefit Calculators:

In addition to the Retirement Estimator, the SSA offers a variety of other benefit calculators designed to help you estimate your potential Social Security benefits. These calculators cover a range of scenarios, including disability benefits, survivor benefits, and spousal benefits. By inputting relevant information about your work history, age, and family situation, you can get a better understanding of the benefits you may be eligible for and how much you can expect to receive.

My Social Security Account:

Another invaluable online tool provided by the SSA is the My Social Security account. This secure online portal allows you to access your Social Security information anytime, anywhere. From checking your earnings record and estimating your benefits to updating your personal information and applying for benefits online, My Social Security puts the power of Social Security management in your hands. By creating an account and logging in regularly, you can stay informed about your benefits and make sure your information is up to date.

Retirement Planning Tools:

In addition to the tools offered directly by the SSA, there are also a variety of third-party retirement planning tools available online. These tools often provide more comprehensive retirement planning features, allowing you to factor in other sources of income, such as pensions and savings accounts, and explore different retirement scenarios in greater detail. By using these tools in conjunction with the SSA's online resources, you can gain a more holistic view of your retirement outlook and make more informed decisions about your financial future.

12.3 Local Assistance and Support Services

While online tools and calculators can be incredibly helpful, sometimes nothing beats the personal touch of local assistance and support services. Whether you're struggling to navigate the Social Security system, facing challenges with your benefits application, or simply seeking guidance on retirement planning, there are a variety of local resources available to help you every step of the way.

Social Security Offices:

One of the most valuable resources for Social Security beneficiaries is their local Social Security office. Staffed by knowledgeable professionals, these offices can provide personalized assistance with a wide range of Social Security-related issues, including benefit applications, appeals, and general inquiries. Whether you prefer to schedule an appointment in person or speak with someone over the phone, your local Social Security office is there to help.

Aging and Disability Resource Centers:

In addition to Social Security offices, many communities also have Aging and Disability Resource Centers (ADRCs) that offer a variety of services to seniors and individuals with disabilities. These centers often provide information and assistance on a range of topics, including Social Security benefits, Medicare enrollment, long-term care options, and more. By reaching out to your local ADRC, you can access a wealth of resources and support to help you navigate the complexities of aging and disability.

Nonprofit Organizations and Advocacy Groups:

Finally, don't overlook the valuable support provided by nonprofit organizations and advocacy groups focused on Social Security issues. From legal aid organizations that can help you navigate the appeals process to advocacy groups that work to protect and expand Social Security benefits for all Americans, there are a variety of organizations dedicated to supporting Social Security beneficiaries and ensuring they receive the benefits they deserve. By connecting with these organizations, you can access additional resources and support to help you navigate the Social Security system and advocate for your rights.

In conclusion, while online tools and calculators can be incredibly helpful for navigating the Social Security system, don't underestimate the value of local assistance and support services. By taking advantage of these resources, you can get personalized guidance and support to help you make informed decisions about your benefits and ensure you're receiving the assistance you deserve.

13. Glossary of Social Security Terms

Understanding the terminology used in Social Security can be essential for navigating the complexities of the program. Below are some key terms and definitions to help you better understand Social Security:

13.1 Key Terminology and Definitions

1. Social Security Administration (SSA):

- The federal agency responsible for administering Social Security benefits and programs.

2. Retirement Benefits:

- Monthly payments provided to individuals who have reached retirement age and have paid into the Social Security system through payroll taxes.

3. Full Retirement Age (FRA):

- The age at which individuals become eligible to receive full retirement benefits. FRA varies depending on the year of birth.

4. Primary Insurance Amount (PIA):

- The monthly benefit amount a person is entitled to receive at full retirement age, based on their lifetime earnings record.

5. Disability Benefits:

- Monthly payments provided to individuals who are unable to work due to a qualifying disability.

6. Social Security Disability Insurance (SSDI):

- A program that provides disability benefits to individuals who have earned enough work credits and meet the Social Security Administration's definition of disability.

7. Supplemental Security Income (SSI):

- A program that provides financial assistance to low-income individuals who are aged, blind, or disabled.

8. Survivor Benefits:

- Monthly payments provided to the surviving spouses, children, and other dependents of deceased workers who were covered by Social Security.

9. Spousal Benefits:

- Monthly payments provided to the spouses of retired, disabled, or deceased workers who are eligible for Social Security benefits.

10. Dependent Benefits:

- Monthly payments provided to certain family members of retired, disabled, or deceased workers who are eligible for Social Security benefits.

11. Work Credits:

- Units used to measure a person's eligibility for Social Security benefits. Individuals earn work credits based on their earnings from work covered by Social Security.

12. Earnings Record:

- A record of an individual's earnings from work covered by Social Security. The earnings record is used to calculate Social Security benefits.

13. Full-Time Student:

- An individual who is enrolled in an accredited educational institution and is attending classes on a full-time basis.

14. Cost-of-Living Adjustment (COLA):

- An annual adjustment to Social Security benefits to account for inflation and changes in the cost of living.

15. Retirement Earnings Test:

- A test that applies to individuals who are receiving Social Security benefits and working before reaching full retirement age. Earnings above a certain limit may result in a reduction of benefits.

16. Lump-Sum Death Payment:

- A one-time payment made to the surviving spouse or eligible family members of a deceased worker who was covered by Social Security.

17. Windfall Elimination Provision (WEP):

- A provision that may reduce the Social Security benefits of individuals who receive pensions from work not covered by Social Security.

18. Government Pension Offset (GPO):

- A provision that may reduce the Social Security benefits of individuals who receive spousal or survivor benefits and also receive a pension from government employment not covered by Social Security.

19. Representative Payee:

- An individual or organization appointed by the Social Security Administration to manage Social Security benefits on behalf of someone who is unable to manage their own finances.

20. My Social Security Account:

- An online portal provided by the Social Security Administration that allows individuals to access their Social Security information, including benefit statements, earnings records, and estimated benefit amounts.

Understanding these key terms and definitions can help you navigate the Social Security system with confidence and make informed decisions about your benefits. If you have any questions about specific terms or need further clarification, don't hesitate to reach out to a Social Security advisor or visit the Social Security Administration's website for additional information.

14. Conclusion

In conclusion, navigating the complexities of Social Security can be a daunting task, but armed with knowledge and understanding, you can make informed decisions about your financial future. Throughout this guide, we've explored the various aspects of Social Security, from its inception during the Great Depression to its evolution into one of the most successful social programs in American history.

14.1 Recap of Key Learnings

Let's recap some of the key learnings from our journey through Social Security:

1. **Understanding Social Security Benefits:** We've learned about the different types of Social Security benefits available, including retirement benefits, disability benefits, survivor benefits, spousal benefits, and dependent benefits. Each benefit type serves a unique purpose and has specific eligibility criteria.

2. **Eligibility and Enrollment**: We've discussed the eligibility criteria for each benefit type, emphasizing the

importance of earning enough work credits and meeting the Social Security Administration's definition of disability.

3. Online Tools and Calculators: We've explored the various online tools and calculators offered by the Social Security Administration, such as the Retirement Estimator and My Social Security account, which can help you estimate your benefits and manage your Social Security information.

4. Local Assistance and Support Services: We've highlighted the importance of seeking assistance from local Social Security offices, Aging and Disability Resource Centers, and nonprofit organizations for personalized guidance and support.

5. Key Terminology and Definitions: We've provided a glossary of key Social Security terms and definitions to help you better understand the language of Social Security and navigate the system with confidence.

By empowering yourself with knowledge and taking advantage of available resources, you can make the most of Social Security benefits and ensure a more secure financial future for yourself and your loved ones. Remember, Social Security is more than just a government program – it's a promise to uphold the dignity and well-being of every American, regardless of age, income, or circumstance.

As you continue your journey with Social Security, don't hesitate to reach out to qualified professionals or utilize online resources for further assistance. With careful planning and informed decision-making, you can navigate the complexities of Social Security with confidence and peace of mind.

14.2 Planning for a Secure Social Security Future

As we conclude our discussion on Social Security, it's essential to emphasize the importance of planning for a secure future. Social Security is a critical component of many Americans' retirement income, but it's just one piece of the puzzle. To ensure financial security in retirement, it's essential to take a proactive approach to retirement planning.

Start Early:

One of the most important steps you can take to secure your Social Security future is to start planning early. The earlier you begin saving and investing for retirement, the more time your money has to grow. Consider contributing to retirement accounts such as 401(k)s, IRAs, or other employer-sponsored plans to supplement your Social Security benefits.

Maximize Your Earnings:

Since Social Security benefits are based on your lifetime earnings, maximizing your income throughout your career can lead to higher benefits in retirement. Consider opportunities for career advancement, additional training or education, or even starting a side business to boost your earning potential.

Understand Your Benefits:

Take the time to understand how Social Security benefits are calculated and how different claiming strategies can impact your benefits. Consider factors such as your full retirement age, the impact of early or delayed claiming, and potential spousal or survivor benefits. By maximizing your benefits and making informed decisions about when to claim, you can optimize your Social Security income.

Diversify Your Income:

While Social Security provides a valuable source of retirement income, it's essential to diversify your income sources to reduce risk and increase financial security. Explore other sources of retirement income, such as pensions, annuities, investment accounts, and rental income, to create a well-rounded retirement portfolio.

Consider Long-Term Care:

As you plan for retirement, don't forget to consider the potential costs of long-term care. Health care expenses can be a significant drain on retirement savings, so it's essential to plan ahead and explore options for long-term care insurance or other strategies to mitigate these costs.

Stay Informed:

Finally, stay informed about changes to the Social Security program and evolving retirement planning strategies. Keep up to date with the latest news and developments in retirement planning, and consider seeking guidance from qualified financial advisors or Social Security experts to ensure you're making the most of your benefits.

By taking a proactive approach to retirement planning and optimizing your Social Security benefits, you can create a secure and fulfilling future for yourself and your loved ones. Remember, the key to a successful retirement is planning ahead, staying informed, and taking action to achieve your financial goals. Here's to a bright and secure Social Security future!

Appreciation

We extend our heartfelt gratitude to all those who contributed to the creation of this guide on Social Security.

First and foremost, we would like to thank the Social Security Administration for providing valuable resources and information that served as the foundation for this guide. Your dedication to serving the American people and upholding the principles of Social Security is truly commendable.

We also express our appreciation to the countless experts, advisors, and professionals in the field of Social Security who generously shared their knowledge and insights. Your expertise and guidance have been invaluable in crafting a comprehensive and informative resource for individuals seeking to navigate the complexities of Social Security.

Additionally, we extend our thanks to the writers, editors, and contributors who dedicated their time and effort to research, write, and refine the content of this guide. Your commitment to excellence and attention to detail have ensured that this guide is informative, accurate, and accessible to readers of all backgrounds.

Last but certainly not least, we express our gratitude to the readers and users of this guide. Your interest, engagement, and feedback are the driving force behind our efforts to provide valuable resources and information on Social Security. Thank you for entrusting us to be a part of your journey toward a secure financial future.

Together, we strive to empower individuals with the knowledge and resources they need to make informed decisions about their Social Security benefits and plan for a brighter tomorrow. Thank you for your support and participation in this important endeavor.

With sincere appreciation,

"Elysian Sage"